W9-CLX-808

THE
NEW ORLEANS
LEVEE FAILURE

BY EMMA HUDDLESTON

CONTENT CONSULTANT
Robert Verchick, JD
Gauthier-St. Martin Chair in Environmental Law
Loyola University New Orleans

Core Library

An Imprint of Abdo Publishing
abdobooks.com

Cover image: Rescue crews used helicopters to help fly
people to safety after Hurricane Katrina.

abdobooks.com

Published by Abdo Publishing, a division of ABDO, PO Box 398166,
Minneapolis, Minnesota 55439. Copyright © 2020 by Abdo Consulting
Group, Inc. International copyrights reserved in all countries. No part of this
book may be reproduced in any form without written permission from the
publisher. Core Library™ is a trademark and logo of Abdo Publishing.

Printed in the United States of America, North Mankato, Minnesota
092019
012020

THIS BOOK CONTAINS
RECYCLED MATERIALS

Cover Photo: Vincent Laforet/Pool/AFP/Getty Images
Interior Photos: Vincent Laforet/Pool/AFP/Getty Images, 1, 29; NOAA/Getty Images News/Getty
Images, 4–5, 43; Red Line Editorial, 8, 20; Photo12/UIG/Universal Images Group/Getty Images,
12–13; Bill Allen/AP Images, 16; Corey Sipkin/NY Daily News Archive/Getty Images, 18–19; Mario
Tama/Getty Images News/Getty Images, 22, 37, 39; Lieut. Commander Mark Moran/NOAA Corps/
NMAO/AOC/NOAA, 25; Jerry Grayson/Helifilms Australia PTY Ltd/Getty Images News/Getty
Images, 26–27, 45; Linda Rosier/NY Daily News Archive/Getty Images, 31; Julie Dermansky/Corbis
News/Getty Images, 34–35

Editor: Marie Pearson
Series Designer: Ryan Gale

Library of Congress Control Number: 2019942093

Publisher's Cataloging-in-Publication Data

Names: Huddleston, Emma, author.
Title: The New Orleans levee failure / by Emma Huddleston
Description: Minneapolis, Minnesota : Abdo Publishing, 2020 | Series: Engineering disasters |
    Includes online resources and index.
Identifiers: ISBN 9781532190742 (lib. bdg.) | ISBN 9781532176593 (ebook)
Subjects: LCSH: Dikes (Engineering)--Juvenile literature. | Disasters--Juvenile literature. |
    Engineering--Juvenile literature. | Dam safety--Juvenile | New Orleans (La.)--History--
    Juvenile literature.
Classification: DDC 363.3493 --dc23

CONTENTS

CHAPTER ONE

A CITY DESTROYED

Strong winds blew outside. Rain hammered the streets. Hurricane Katrina arrived on the southern US coast in August 2005. The city of New Orleans, Louisiana, was hit on August 29. The storm did not hit the city directly. But it did a lot of damage. It was a day people would not forget.

New Orleans had a flood protection system. It had both levees and floodwalls. These are physical barriers created to direct water away from people and cities during storms. Floodwalls are made of concrete. Levees are compacted rock and soil.

A satellite image shows Hurricane Katrina approaching Louisiana.

Lakes Pontchartrain and Borgne are in New Orleans. Despite their names, both are lagoons, meaning they connect with the sea. The levee and floodwall system was made to control water flowing from the sea into these lagoons. However, the lakes filled up during Katrina. They held an additional 10 inches (25 cm) of rainwater. Then the storm surge came. A storm surge is when when wind pushes seawater toward shore. This causes water levels to rise. Waves rose to 19 feet (5.8 m) high. The Industrial Canal levee showed

HURRICANE SCALE

The Saffir-Simpson scale categorizes hurricanes by wind speed. The categories are 1 through 5. Categories 1 and 2 have winds at speeds of 74 to 110 miles per hour (119–177 km/h). Hurricanes with winds more than 110 miles per hour (177 km/h) are considered major storms. They include categories 3 to 5. Hurricane Katrina was a category 3 when it hit land. The storm brought winds blowing at 100 to 140 miles per hour (160–225 km/h). It stretched 400 miles (640 km) across.

weakness first. Then the flood protection system failed. Water poured over the tops of some levees. Other levees broke, and water rushed into the city.

Hurricane Katrina hit New Orleans early in the morning. Winds were as strong as 125 miles per hour (200 km/h). Tree branches and parts of buildings blew away. More levees and floodwalls failed. Water rushed down the streets. Cars went underwater. People climbed to their roofs for safety in the Ninth Ward, a neighborhood in the city. New Orleans flooded. It was a disaster.

The levee at the London Avenue Canal was the last major breach. A breach is an area that has been broken through. It added to the damage already done. Homes were flooded. Water levels in the streets were up to 13 feet (4 m) deep. Katrina only raged in New Orleans for a few hours. But by August 30, 80 percent of the city was underwater.

NEW ORLEANS MAP

Most of New Orleans was flooded after Hurricane Katrina. How does this map help you understand the storm and its impact in a new way?

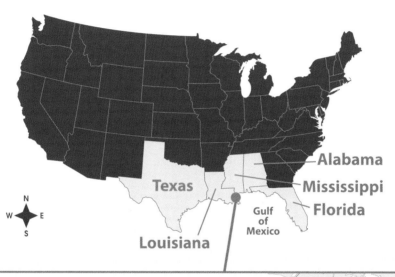

Alabama

Mississippi

Florida

Texas

Gulf of Mexico

Louisiana

N
W E
S

New Orleans

Lake Pontchartrain

17th Street Canal

Lakefront Airport

Industrial Canal

London Avenue Canal

Lower Ninth Ward

Lake Borgne

Superdome

Mississippi River

AFTER THE STORM

The first few days after the storm were quiet. The wind was gone. Birds and insects were silent. The lack of sound seemed unnatural. Katrina did more damage than people expected. City leaders had warned people to evacuate. But many stayed. Some did not have a car. Others wanted to wait in their homes. This left more than 60,000 people stranded for many days.

The National Guard saved more than 30,000 people. Helicopters flew over the city. Their crews spotted people on rooftops. Cardboard posters had messages calling for help. Some residents waved their arms in the air.

Katrina's impact on New Orleans was not over when the storm ended. It took a huge toll on the city. The storm caused hundreds of billions of dollars of damage. Across five southern states, more than 1,800 people died. More than 86 percent of the people who lost their lives lived in Louisiana. Some people

HEROES IN THE FLOOD

In the weeks after the flood, thousands of people needed help. They were trapped in flooded homes. This caused regular people to become heroes. They rescued others by boat. Kenny Bellau was one of these heroes. He originally got on a boat to save his cat. Then he realized a bigger mission was needed. On the boat he said, "Every living thing. We are going to bring every living thing with us." Bellau's boat was 24 feet (7.3 m) long. He drove it for two weeks. He helped save more than 400 people and many pets. Now his boat is on display in New Orleans.

had to live in cramped temporary housing. Bacteria grew in the warm floodwaters.

New Orleans was spared a direct hit from the storm, but the storm uncovered a bigger threat. The levee system built to hold back water was completely overwhelmed. It failed in more than 50 spots. Many people wondered what went wrong.

STRAIGHT TO THE
SOURCE

Ivor van Heerden is a hurricane expert. He and his team saw the possibility of tragedy in New Orleans years before Katrina hit:

Louisiana is a terminally ill patient requiring major surgery, a patient that if it was given a new heart and new lungs and a new liver would live. If it isn't, it's going to die. . . .

So just imagine, you've got this super, super crowding—highly, highly stressed folk. They don't have a home. They don't have a job. They don't see any future. They're living in tents. It's hot, humid Louisiana. And now you have the potential of disease.

These are some of the worst-case scenarios. We will have almost a million displaced persons that are going to be totally dependent on the state. . . . And it's going to require a massive operation to try and bring some normality into these people's lives.

Source: "The Man Who Predicted Katrina." *NOVA PBS*. WGBH Educational Foundation, November 21, 2005. Web. Accessed March 27, 2019.

What's the Big Idea?
In this passage, van Heerden compares the state of Louisiana to a patient needing medical care. What is the main idea of the passage? Name two or three details that support it.

CHAPTER
TWO

LIVING NEAR WATER

New Orleans has a rich history. Native Americans, including the Chitimacha and Atakapa, first lived in the area. Then the French founded the city of New Orleans in 1718. Later it was under Spanish rule before becoming a US state in 1803. It combined cultures from around the world to become a vibrant city.

New Orleans is the largest city in Louisiana. The Mississippi River flows through it to the Gulf of Mexico. New Orleans is 110 miles (177 km) from the mouth of the river. This location is part of what encouraged

New Orleans has long been an important port city.

THE PORT CITY

New Orleans is a major port in the United States for many reasons. Its location on the water is ideal for trade and industry. Some major products it exports are grains, oils, fabrics, animal feed, and coal. Many imported goods come into the country through the city too. Each year, approximately 5,000 ocean vessels from other countries dock at New Orleans. Many factories in the city produce more resources for trade. These include food, clothing, stone, glass, and metal items. The port city is also used for different kinds of transportation. It is home to three airports, several railroads, and many buses, trucks, and ships.

people to settle there throughout history. Ships used the port for trade and business. This helped make New Orleans a busy and successful place to live.

HIGH SEA LEVELS

Life in New Orleans includes dealing with water. Sea levels in the United States have been rising for decades. Scientists say that sea levels around the world will rise 3 to 6 feet (1–2 m) by the year 2100. Rising waters can cause problems for people living near the coast.

Many things about New Orleans put it at risk of flooding. The city gets an average annual rainfall of 57 inches (145 cm). Lake Pontchartrain can flood if the rain doesn't drain quickly enough or if there is a storm surge. And parts of the city are 5 to 10 feet (1.5–3 m) below sea level.

FLOOD PROTECTION

New Orleans needed protection from flooding. The US Army Corps of Engineers (USACE) built levees and floodwalls in New Orleans during the 1900s. Levees and floodwalls are physical barriers. They have been used for thousands of years.

PERSPECTIVES

WHY I LIVE IN NEW ORLEANS

Mike Karney played on the New Orleans Saints football team before and after Katrina. He remembered difficult times: "We took it upon ourselves to be the shining light for the city. It needed to be a positive restart to the city for everything [the people] went through. . . . We felt inspired from them as well. That '06 season will always be one of the greatest things for me to be a part of."

A 1946 photo shows a New Orleans levee along the Mississippi River holding the water back from homes.

Both types of barriers control water by directing it away from people and cities. But the structures are slightly different.

Levees are made of natural materials such as dirt, sand, clay, and rocks. The earthy materials are compacted together. This forms an earthen ridge along a body of water. Levees work in pairs. One goes on either side of the water source to direct the way water flows. Floodwalls are often made of concrete. They can stand alone or be built on top of a levee. They can be 1 to 20 feet (0.3–6 m) tall. They block water from flowing into an area. However, the barriers weren't enough when the time came to stand up against Katrina's surge.

EXPLORE ONLINE

Chapter Two talks about levees. The website below also has information about levees. What information is the same? What new information did the website have?

NATIONAL GEOGRAPHIC: LEVEE

abdocorelibrary.com/new-orleans-levee-failure

THE DISASTER

Hurricane Katrina started as a tropical storm in the Bahamas. It grew into a hurricane on August 25, 2005. The Gulf of Mexico has warm waters. The storm gained strength there. It doubled in size. Winds blew faster. At one point, they reached speeds of 170 miles per hour (275 km/h). Katrina raged from August 23 to August 31. It made landfall southeast of New Orleans on August 29. When the storm surge struck the city, it was devastating.

The storm did more damage than some predicted. It affected relief organizations' ability to get supplies to

Many people stayed home during Hurricane Katrina because their pets weren't allowed in emergency shelters.

KATRINA
TIMELINE

Hurricane Katrina started as a tropical storm, grew into a hurricane, and shrank when it hit land. At what point was Katrina the strongest?

1. **August 23, 2:00 p.m. Eastern Time:** a tropical depression forms

2. **August 24, 8:00 a.m.:** Katrina becomes a tropical storm

3. **August 24, 8:00 p.m.:** tropical storm

4. **August 25, 8:00 p.m.:** category 1 hurricane

5. **August 26, 8:00 p.m.:** category 2 hurricane

6. **August 27, 8:00 p.m.,** category 3 hurricane

7. **August 28, 8:00 p.m.:** category 5 hurricane

8. **August 29, 8:00 a.m.,** category 3 hurricane

9. **August 29, 8:00 p.m.:** tropical storm

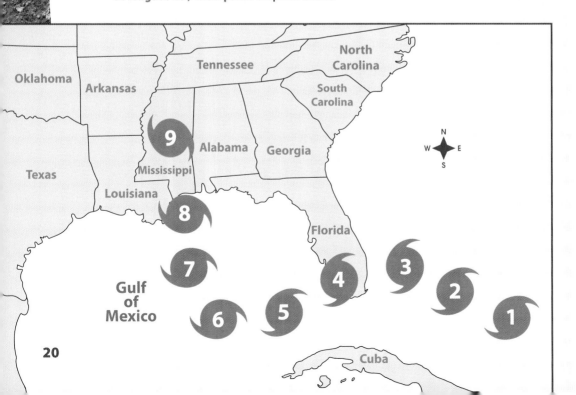

the Superdome. This sports stadium was one of the places where people in New Orleans took refuge. By September 1, approximately 30,000 people were there. The Superdome was crowded. It was dirty and lacked food and safe water. It was not prepared to help the number of people who were displaced.

RECOVERY

Some experts say the government's response to the flooding could have been faster and more effective. Still, many government workers provided important assistance in the days following the disaster. They made preparations and packed supplies. On September 2, National Guard troops arrived in New Orleans. They rescued more than 33,500 people. More than 9,000 needed medical help right away. The US Coast Guard also helped save lives. Its rescue and response efforts after Katrina were some of the largest in its history. More than 5,600 Coast Guard workers helped people after this disaster. At one point, the Coast Guard

Government workers rescued many people after Katrina.

rescued 750 people by boat and 100 people by air in one hour.

The government plays an important role in disaster recovery. It gives emergency money to help rebuild. Government workers such as members of the Coast Guard rushed to rescue people and care for their injuries after Katrina. Red Cross volunteers came from Texas. Search boats looked for people stranded in their homes. Volunteers cleared debris from roads. They delivered food, water, and clothing. Levees were rebuilt. The last floodwater was pumped out of the city on October 11. That was 43 days after Katrina made landfall.

THE TOLL

The storm killed more than 1,800 people. Most of those who died were at least 60 years old. Additionally, 600,000 pets became homeless or died. Financially, Katrina was the costliest natural disaster in US history.

CHANGES IN DIVERSITY AFTER KATRINA

In 2015, nearly 100,000 fewer African American people lived in New Orleans than before the hurricane. After the storm, many people moved away. Other populations grew after the storm. More Hispanic people moved into the city. Many of them came because of the new job openings. The city needed more workers to rebuild. People stayed because they found work. The Hispanic population grew by 2 percent, or 6,000 people.

THE ROLE OF MONEY IN RECOVERY

Professor Craig Colten studied how Katrina affected the population of New Orleans. Before Katrina, people with money lived in high areas. Low-lying areas were cheaper but more at risk for flooding. Colten found that "class and wealth do play a big part of people's ability to respond. And certainly, those people with the least means lose everything." After Katrina, some people didn't have cars or couldn't afford to leave. They were left with damaged homes and buildings. As a result of the smaller population, the city had less money to rebuild.

Hurricane Harvey hit Texas in 2017, and it was ranked second. Harvey caused more than $125 billion in damage. Katrina caused more than $161 billion in damage.

Floodwaters washed away homes. Rubble spread out for miles. Afterward, 300,000 homes were unlivable. The city's economy was hurt. The port had $260 million in damage. Sugar crops normally brought in $500 million each year. Farmers lost 40 percent

Hurricane Katrina left entire neighborhoods underwater.

of the crop to the storm. Tourism for the city was less than half the normal amount.

Businesses closed. More than 400,000 people had fled during the disaster. Many did not return. The population of New Orleans dropped by 29 percent during the next six years.

WHAT WENT WRONG?

The disaster led people to investigate the flood protection system. They wanted to know why it failed in more than 50 places. What people found was shocking. The flood protection system failure in New Orleans was widespread. Many people reviewed the ways in which the levees and floodwalls failed. New Orleans had 284 miles (457 km) of federal levees and floodwalls standing before Katrina. Of that, 169 miles (272 km) were damaged.

Scientists and engineers looked into the reasons for the breaches between

A breach in the London Avenue Canal allowed water to flood a neighborhood.

SCIENTISTS MAP DAMAGE

Researchers Robert Kayen and Brian Collins were in New Orleans from October 9 through October 14 after Katrina. Kayen said, "Both Brian and I are familiar with post-event [earthquake] damage, but the devastation of Hurricane Katrina was so unusually severe . . . that we were taken aback by the magnitude of this natural and manmade catastrophe." They collected details about the levee breaches. They recorded data on soil level, levee height, depth of erosion, and damage done to barriers still standing.

September 28 and October 15. Then emergency repairs needed to be done.

REASONS FOR BREACHES

The most common reason for levee failure was due to overtopping. This is when water rises over the barrier. In addition, the water scoured out, or washed away, the ground on the other side. This ground helps support the barriers. Without it, the barriers

Water rushes over the Industrial Canal levee, flooding the Lower Ninth Ward.

are weaker. A simple way to protect against scouring is to extend a slab of concrete out from the base of the wall. Water does not easily break down concrete like it can dirt. The combination of overtopping and scouring led to failure.

Reviews also found weakness at many transition points. Transition points are where levees or floodwalls of different heights and materials meet. The levee at the Lakefront Airport was vulnerable for two reasons. It was a transition point, and it did not have scour protection.

Weak foundations caused three major breaches. This happened because of peat soil or erosion. Peat soil is mushy material often found in swamps and marshes. It is not reliable for supporting any structures. Some levees were built on peat soil. Erosion can happen over time. Water flows through rivers and can shift materials meant to support pylons. Weak foundations caused levee failures at the London Avenue and 17th Street

Engineering mistakes caused widespread destruction in New Orleans, especially in the Lower Ninth Ward.

Canals. These levees failed before water heights reached the top.

STRUCTURE DESIGN MISTAKES

The deeper reason behind these failures went back to the system's design. Researchers discovered that the USACE made many mistakes when it first built the barriers. In some areas, the soil was not as strong as thought. Engineers did not realize or did not take into account sandy, swampy, or loose peat soil. Structures in these areas should have had more pylons for strength and stability.

The USACE designed the flood protection system for a standard hurricane in New Orleans. During the

1900s, these storms were less severe than Katrina. Barriers at Lake Pontchartrain were built for wind speeds of 100 miles per hour (160 km/h). But stronger storms became more common. After some barriers were built, the National Weather Service updated data about standard hurricanes in New Orleans. They could now reach wind speeds up to 160 miles per hour (260 km/h). The USACE failed to change the barriers.

Many of the levees and floodwalls were not strong enough

WHAT TO CONSIDER WHEN BUILDING BARRIERS

Building barriers for flood protection is complicated. Engineers must consider many things. The height of the barrier is determined by location and soil type. Taller barriers need more space. They also need strong and supportive soil. If water seeps easily into the soil, the barrier could be washed away. Drains and sump pumps can remove water from under or inside a barrier. The costs of building and maintaining the barrier are also important. Costs depend on materials and the time workers spend there.

because the USACE built them based on storms that were weaker than average for the area. Additionally, they used designs just barely strong enough to hold back those weaker storms. Some levees were 2 feet (0.6 m) shorter than they should have been. The Industrial Canal levee was one of the barriers that was too short.

The flaws in the New Orleans levee system were caused by engineers' decisions that left weak structures. Failing to update project plans and choosing not to properly maintain the system threatened the public's safety.

FURTHER EVIDENCE

Chapter Four explains some of the reasons the New Orleans barriers failed during Katrina. What was one of the main points of this chapter? What evidence is used to support the point? Look at the website below. Find a quote that supports the chapter's main point.

DOSOMETHING.ORG: 11 FACTS ABOUT HURRICANE KATRINA
abdocorelibrary.com/new-orleans-levee-failure

LEARNING FROM MISTAKES

The city of New Orleans and the US government put time, money, and effort into preventing future floods. By 2015, they had spent $14.5 billion to build stronger levees and floodwalls. They made 133 miles (214 km) of levees topped with concrete floodwalls. A massive surge barrier was built at Lake Borgne. This type of barrier has gates that can be closed when a storm surge hits. It protects approximately 1 million people, including those in the Lower Ninth Ward. It is 26 feet (7.9 m) tall and 2 miles (3.2 km) long. It cost $1.1 billion.

The new surge barrier has gates that allow ships through but can be closed to seal off the city from a storm surge.

The USACE designed these new levees carefully. It used computer technology to simulate 152 types of hurricanes. This let it test different models and ideas. It created better design plans. Louisiana also spent money to prevent flooding problems. This included raising buildings above sea level.

New Orleans is at more risk as time goes on. Coastal wetlands are being destroyed. Wetlands are marshy areas. They are natural storm buffers because they take in the first waves of water and strong storm winds. They are known as the "green" part of

BUILT FOR BIGGER STORMS

The USACE built a strong new levee system in New Orleans. The system had to handle fairly strong hurricanes that have a 1 percent chance of happening in the area each year. But protective wetlands are still being destroyed and climate change is causing sea levels to rise. As soon as 2023, the system might not be able to handle a 1-percent storm. A review found that 80 percent of the new levees were at high risk of failing from a storm smaller than Katrina.

Louisiana is losing its wetlands because people are not caring for them.

the New Orleans flood system. They work together with the "gray" part, which includes floodwalls and levees made by humans. Without the green, the gray would fail. Both parts of the flood system need to be cared for.

The coastal wetlands in New Orleans make up 40 percent of all coastal wetlands in the lower 48 states. In order to preserve them, Louisiana plans to spend $50 billion to restore the coast, but the state will not pay for it on its own. All Americans benefit from having a healthy coast, so the state will get money from the federal government. Coastal restoration aims to protect nature on the coast. Scientists monitor the water to make sure it is clean enough to support plants and animals. They also bring plants and animals that normally live there back to the area.

NEW SAFETY SYSTEMS

The Westbank area used to have gaps in the floodwall system. After Katrina, these gaps were filled with new, stronger barriers. Floodwalls and levees went from an average of 8 feet (2.4 m) tall to 12 feet (3.7 m) tall. T-walls are a type of sturdy floodwall. They are shaped like an upside-down T. The shape protects against scouring. They are made of concrete. Pylons underneath each side support the structure.

The West Closure Complex includes a massive pump station. It is the largest in the world. It can pump more than 660,000 gallons (2.5 million L) in 3 seconds. The complex also has a $2 million safe house.

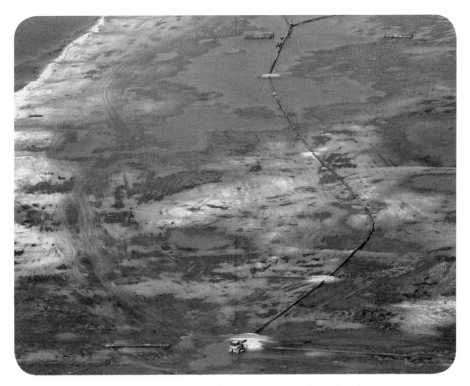

Today, some people are creating more wetlands along Louisiana's coast. They prepare the soil to help wetland plants grow.

The building is for employees and first responders. It protects people responsible for checking the levees and pump systems during a storm. This will allow them to respond quickly.

MAKING ETHICAL DECISIONS

Katrina led people to realize engineers' great responsibility. It was a reminder that people's

BETTER THAN BEFORE

Michael Hecht was a business owner in New Orleans after Katrina. He said, "There's been a massive investment in new infrastructure, in roads, in schools, and the hospital, that are supporting the economy post-Katrina. . . . The way that you honor the loss from disaster is by rebuilding something better." Ten years after Katrina, he noticed a special effort behind people's work. They wanted to restore the city in honor of the people who died.

lives depend on their work. Disasters like Katrina have shown it is important to speak up. Instead of keeping quiet about risky or vulnerable areas, engineers are encouraged to let the public know.

People are learning from the past. They are taking extra care in creating future safety systems. City leaders want to protect New Orleans from future disasters. The people living there rebuilt their lives. They didn't let flooding wash away the vibrant spirit of life in New Orleans.

STRAIGHT TO THE
SOURCE

Tara Hoke works for the American Society of Civil Engineers (ASCE). She wrote an article about the ethical lessons learned from the New Orleans levee failure after Katrina. She said:

> *Nevertheless, if the engineer's ethical duty is to hold paramount the safety, health, and welfare of the public, then the Katrina disaster demonstrates the costs of failing to be vigilant in honoring that duty. As the persons best qualified by education and experience to understand the ramifications of technical decisions, it is essential that engineers question decisions that compromise safety or reliability and that they clearly communicate risks and consequences when they believe a course of action poses too great a threat to the public.*

Source: "The Lessons of Katrina." *ASCE*. ASCE, July 1, 2015. Web. Accessed March 27, 2019.

Consider Your Audience

Review this passage closely. Consider how you would adapt it for a different audience, such as your younger friends. Write a blog post conveying this same information for the new audience. How does your new approach differ from the original text, and why?

FAST FACTS

- Hurricane Katrina hit New Orleans on August 29, 2005. It flooded 80 percent of the city.

- Because of Katrina, more than 1,800 people died, most in New Orleans. The hurricane also caused $161 billion worth of damage.

- The levee and floodwall protection system in New Orleans failed in 50 locations during the storm.

- Some reasons for the levee and floodwall failures included overtopping and scouring, weak foundation material, and poor structure design.

- After the storm, Louisiana, with the help of the federal government, built a $14.5 billion levee and floodwall system that was stronger than the first. It also made plans to restore and preserve the coastal wetlands.

- The American Society for Civil Engineering's Code of Ethics explains engineers' responsibilities. Smart choices can keep people safe; bad choices can put people's lives in danger.

STOP AND
THINK

Tell the Tale
Chapter Two of this book discusses living near water. Imagine you live in a place that gets hurricanes. Write 200 words about why you live there even though the weather can be challenging. How does your city or state help protect people?

Dig Deeper
After reading this book, what questions do you still have about flood prevention? With an adult's help, find a few reliable sources that can help you answer your questions. Write a paragraph about what you learned.

Say What?
Studying engineering means learning a lot of new vocabulary. Find five words in this book you've never heard before. Use a dictionary to find out what they mean. Then write the meanings in your own words, and use each word in a new sentence.

Another View

This book talks about the impact of Hurricane Katrina.
As you know, every source is different. Ask a librarian or
another adult to help you find another source about this
event. Write a short essay comparing and contrasting
the new source's point of view with that of this book's
author. What is the point of view of each author?
How are they similar and why? How are they
different and why?

GLOSSARY

compacted
packed closely together

debris
pieces of garbage or
wreckage from a storm or
other natural disaster

displaced
forced to flee from
one's home

erosion
the process of
breaking down

evacuate
to leave someplace quickly
and urgently

export
to sell to or trade with
another place, typically to
another country

pylon
a stiff beam in the ground
that supports levees
and floodwalls

simulate
to copy a situation in order
to test it

tourism
when people travel to places
for fun

ONLINE
RESOURCES

To learn more about the New Orleans levee failure, visit our free resource websites below.

Core Library
CONNECTION
FREE! COMMON CORE MULTIMEDIA RESOURCES

Visit **abdocorelibrary.com** or scan this QR code for free Common Core resources for teachers and students, including vetted activities, multimedia, and booklinks, for deeper subject comprehension.

Booklinks
NONFICTION NETWORK
FREE! ONLINE NONFICTION RESOURCES

Visit **abdobooklinks.com** or scan this QR code for free additional online weblinks for further learning. These links are routinely monitored and updated to provide the most current information available.

LEARN
MORE

Decker, Michael. *New Orleans.* Minneapolis, MN: Abdo Publishing, 2020.

Zullo, Allan. *Heroes of Hurricane Katrina.* New York: Scholastic, 2015.

INDEX

About the Author

Emma Huddleston lives in the Twin Cities with her husband.
She enjoys writing educational books, but she likes reading
novels even more. When she is not writing or reading, she
likes to stay active by running and swing dancing.